Being Attacked in the Dark

An Inspirational Memoir
of Hope, Courage and Overcoming Adversity

Ayak Mithyang

BEING ATTACKED IN THE DARK

An Inspirational Memoir of Hope, Courage, and Overcoming Adversity

Address all inquiries:
Ayak Mithyang
Telephone: 619-843-4812
Email: JustForYouDayCare63@yahoo.com

www.Being AttackedInTheDark.com

ISBN: 978-0-578-31940-7

David Guy Harden PHD Editor
Cover Designer : Merritt Voigtlander
Interior Book Layout: Fusion Creative Works

Every attempt has been made to properly source all quotes.

Printed In The United States of America

First Edition

2 4 6 8 1 0 1 2

"My life is dedicated to helping those children who are living the same hard life I lived before. By providing these children with education and health care, by building schools and health care centers throughout South Sudan, these kids can learn skills and make friends across the world. With your gracious help you can make a difference in the world. Any donations are greatly appreciated."

Just a friendly reminder:

A good woman knows how to control her mouth, how to clean her house, how to take care her kids. She's intelligent, she Love's her man even if he has money or not. She knows how to respect herself in public. She doesn't cry for something that doesn't belong to her, she doesn't rely on anyone to take care of her. She built herself. She makes her own decisions, she doesn't let anyone else to make decisions for her. She loves herself and appreciates her man. She doesn't drink or get drunk in public. She's confident. She prays even when she's broke. She picks herself up when she falls. When she is depressed all night she makes sure she wipes her tears in the morning before her kids see her. She smiles. A good woman goes to work even when her car is broke down. She still catches the bus and makes it to work. She doesn't call it off. She doesn't make excuses.

A good man is allergic to his womans tears. He makes her feel good about herself. He holds her hand in public. He pays attention to his woman, if he sees something wrong he tells her in the way that makes her fall in love with him more. He doesn't give her a reason to be fearful. He cries with her when she's in pain, and a smiles with her when she smiles. He takes care of his house. He covers her when she falls asleep without a blanket. He thinks about her all the time when she's not around. He comes to her when he's down. He supports her decisions. He says thank you to his Queen and compliments her.

CONTENTS

PREFACE

A Brief History of South Sudan and the Dinka People

The Dinka people mostly lived along the Nile including the Abyei Area of the Ngok Dinka on the border between Sudan and South Sudan. The Dinka, noted for their height, are one of the tallest people in Africa and number around 4.5 million which is the largest ethnic tribe in South Sudan.

According to oral traditions, the Dinka originated from the Gezira between the Blue Nile and the White Nile in the east-central region of South Sudan. They were under the kingdom of Alodia from about the 10th to the 16th centuries and then became the center of the Funj Sultanate. Sudan's most powerful rulers, based at Khartoum and along the Nile River, have fought against the inland peoples, such as the Dinka, for centuries. The tribe has been the subject of slave raids, military conflicts and droughts throughout its history.

The Dinka's followed an agro-pastoral lifestyle responding to the periodic flooding and dryness of the area in which they lived. The tribe relied on cattle husbandry as a matter of cultural pride, not for commerce or meat, but as a means to perform festivals, marriage dowries, and rituals including a milk ritual. Most Dinka revere one God, Nhialic, who speaks through spirits that take temporary possession of individuals. These spirits are ancestral totems, seen by anthropologists as nature spirits. When an animal, such as a bull, is sacrificed, the master of the fishing spear describes the issue being faced, the people repeat the issue and acknowledge past sins, then hymns called ox-songs are sung, all misfortunes are given to the animal and the animal is sacrificed. The Dinka people are organized into traditional clans led by hereditary ritual chiefs, "masters of the fishing spear" (*beny bith)*, and a clan royalty with kings and queens, princes and princesses.

Dinka, or as they refer to themselves, *Muonyjang* (singular) and *jieng* (plural), make up one of the branches of the River Lake Nilotes who speak Nilotic languages. The Dinka language is called Thuɔŋjäŋ which simply means *People.* Ayak herself grew up speaking Diniklk a tribal branch of the Dinka language.

Under British rule Sudan was split into Moslem Sudan and African South Sudan. In 1905, after continued raids by the Messiria into Ngok Dinka territory, the British redistricted the nine Ngok Dinka chiefdoms into Kordofan. This protected the Ngok Dinka from raids by the Messiria and helped pacify the area. Northern Arabs were prevented from holding positions of power in the south with its African traditions, and trade was discouraged between the two areas.

In 1946, the British gave in to northern pressure to integrate the two areas bringing South Sudan under Moslem control. When the British left in 1956, they left the status of Abyei unclear. Motivated by exploitation the British supported Sudan over South Sudan and they supported Moslem rulers over African rulers. As a result Sudan imposed Shari'a law on South Sudan, which supported beheadings, amputations, and torture. This led to the First and Second Sudanese Civil Wars. The First War (1958 to 1979) lasted 21 years and the Second war (1983 to 2005) lasted 22 years.

In 1983 a Dinka named Dr. John Garang De Mabior became fed up with the Arab Muslim government in Khartoum that was trying to enforce Moslem law on the Dinka. He formed The Sudan People's Liberation Army and took arms against the government. During the subsequent 21-year civil war, many thousands of Dinka, along with fellow non-Dinka southerners, were massacred by government forces. This civil war kicked off tribal conflicts where the non-Dinka tribes formed militia to defend their own people and then came into conflict with other tribes. In some cases the conflict degenerated into mass exterminations. Since the independence of South Sudan, the Dinka, led by Salva Kiir Mayardit, have also engaged in a civil war with the Nuer and other groups, who accuse them of dictatorial actions.

The Dinka resisted Moslem teachings throughout their history, clinging to their ancient beliefs. However, since 1983 a large number of Dinka people, displaced by war and drought, have converted to Christianity.

When Prime Minister Sadiq al-Mahdi refused to approve a peace plan reached by the Democratic Unionist Party

(DUP) and the Sudan People's Liberation Army (SPLA) in November 1988, the Umma Party and the fundamentalist National Islamic Front (NIF) formed a new government. In February 1989, Prime Minister Sadiq al-Mahdi was forced to form a new government with the DUP, and approved the SPLA/DUP peace plan -- though a constitution was not adopted. The following year a military junta, the Revolutionary Command Council for National Salvation (RCC), replaced the government by a military leadership with a civilian cabinet. The RCC al-Bashir military government banned trade unions, political parties, and other "non-religious" institutions. About 78,000 members of the army, police, and civil administration were purged in order to reshape the government.

In March 1991, a new penal code in Sudan, the Criminal Act of 1991, instituted harsh punishments, including amputations and stoning under Islamic Shari'a law. The Sudan military then captured the SPLA headquarters in Torit. The military with its notorious militia (People's Defense Forces, PDF) also raided villages in South Sudan and the Nuba Mountains. Ethnic violence became widespread, with all sides targeting civilians to destroy the power bases and recruitment centers of their rivals. Those who could, formed self-defense groups, and these were often based on familial and tribal links as these were the only ones most southern people could still rely on. In this way, groups like the Nuer White Army and Dinka *Titweng* ("cattle guard") militias came into existence. Although intended for civilian defense, many of these groups became brutal gangs.

In addition to these military units, there has also been a significant amount of death from warring tribes in the south. Most of the conflict has been between Nuer and Dinka but other ethnic groups have also been involved.

People suspected of disloyalty or rebel sympathies were arrested by the Sudanese Armed Forces and taken to prisons and barracks, where they were tortured and executed. In the *Giada* barracks in Juba, called the "White House," it is rumored that thousands of people were tortured and murdered. On 15 November 1991, the faction of Riek Machar's SPLA-Nasir alongside the Nuer White Army raided Hol, Nyarweng, Twic, Bor and other villages and deliberately killed an estimated 2,000 Dinkas in what has come to be called the "Dinkas Massacre" or "Bor massacre." In addition to the dead, this left thousands wounded and 100,000 people fled the area.

The British, and then the United States, supported Sudan over South Sudan as a ploy to extract oil from Sudan's extensive oil fields. By 2005, roughly 2.5 million people were killed leaving an aftermath of famine and disease. Four million people in South Sudan were displaced and became refugees. The civilian death toll is one of the highest of any war since World War II with numerous human rights violations, including slavery, torture and mass murder. Abyei's boundaries were created in 2005 under the Comprehensive Peace Agreement but following continued disputes that erupted into violence and threatened the CPA, an international arbitration process redrew Abyei's boundaries in 2009 to make it significantly smaller. The continuing war resulted in the independence of South Sudan on 9 July 2011 and it joined the United Nations.

The United States only withdrew support from Sudan when it became obvious that the Sudanese government was supporting terrorist groups.

South Sudan reported to the United Nations that it was at war with seven or more factions who accused the government of not fairly representing and supporting all tribal groups while neglecting development in rural areas. The UN Interim Security Force was deployed to Abyei in 2011 to protect civilians and humanitarian workers. The Nuer White Army warned it would wipe out the Murle and would fight South Sudanese and UN forces sent to the area around Pibor. The Abyei Area, long contested between Sudan and South Sudan, currently has a special administrative status in Sudan and is governed by an Abyei Area Administration. It was due to hold a referendum on whether to join South Sudan or remain part of the Republic of Sudan, but in May 2011 the Sudanese military seized Abyei. Fighting continued in 2012 between Sudan and South Sudan over the border oil fields.

Also, Joseph Kony's Lord's Resistance Army (LRA) continued to operate in South Sudan until 2017.

In July 2017 the NSS government blocked access to major news websites and popular blogs. One month later, an American journalist, Christopher Allen became embedded with the opposition forces in South Sudan and was killed one week later during fighting between government and opposition forces in the Yei River State. Millions of people fled

South Sudan and President Salva Kiir blamed social media propaganda as conspiring against his government.

As of 22 October 2020 the head of UN Peacekeeping told the Security Council that despite the strengthening of the relationship between Sudan and South Sudan, little progress had been made regarding the disputed Abyei region of the Dinka. Attacks against UNISFA personnel and incidents of intercommunal violence, including armed attacks on villages continue. Nevertheless, a peace treaty between several tribal military groups from Darfur was facilitated by South Sudan. Abyei appointed two chief administrators, one from Juba and one from Khartoum. Leaders from the Nginka and Misseriya were supporting the peace effort as UN police were being reduced from 35 to 19 officers. In exchange for cooperation with South Sudan, Sudan expects to receive 15,000 barrels of oil per day. South Sudan produced 350,000 barrels of oil per day pre-conflict and the conflict has reduced production to 150,000 barrels per day. Most of the oil not used locally is sent to Britain.

This is the environment that I was born into. I am a survivor.

I grew up as a Dinka child in the Dinka culture and had essentially no schooling until I immigrated to North Sudan. There I was taught Arabic in a Moslem culture. I only began to learn British English when I immigrated to Egypt and was still very poor in English when I immigrated to the United States. I prefer to write in Arabic and then translate it to English. I speak and understand English fairly well, but still have trouble reading English.

Special Acknowledgements

David Harden, PhD. Editor.

I want to thank David Harden for his kind generosity in donating his time and writing skills to change my story into this book. Thank you.

When I first met David Harden several years ago in Sunday School he was working on several history books and he immediately impressed me with his deep knowledge of gospel doctrines. He always helped me when I had trouble expressing myself in English and was always kind and gentle. When I needed help with this book he immediately came to mind as the perfect person to help.

I want to personally thank David Harden for volunteering literally dozens of hours of his time to help me publish this book.

INTRODUCTION

"There is always a moment in childhood when the door opens and lets the future in."

— Graham Green

All is dark in the peaceful night. Insects are whirring in the nearby forest. Suddenly there is a crash and someone breaks in your door. What would you do if five soldiers broke into your home at 2 o'clock in the morning? You suddenly fear not only for your life but as a baby you have no idea why these violent men are hurting your mother and your father. The shouting scares you but the flashing lights and the stink of these military men is unreal. It is more like a horrible nightmare than reality.

This was not just one incident that happened to one child, but these soldiers killed millions of men, women and children and drove millions more into refugee camps. This horror was worse in South Sudan than any other African country. This is the story of one girl who lived through the horror and survived. I am telling my story in the hope that I can help end this kind of terror worldwide. I am also seeking help in providing aid to the children of my war torn country and every other country in the world where these atrocities happen daily.

The war in South Sudan is not over by any means. The United States and the U.N. were providing aid to northern Sudan until it became obvious that northern Sudan was supporting the Taliban. The United States withdrew support and the U.N. intervention has been reduced to a few negotiators. So my country is still in deep trouble. Before this time the cooperation between the Taliban and the Moslem governments of Sudan and South Sudan was well known to the inhabitants. The Taliban influence supports the extremism being practiced in these countries.

This book is about my experiences, having escaped the country as a refugee. I tell of all the troubles. Now I return each year to provide teachers, schools, doctors and medical facilities for the children still living in war torn South Sudan and anywhere in the world where I can reach out and provide assistance to the youth and children. It is through these children that we can build a better world.

You cannot change the ingrained opinions of people who have been set in their ways for generations. You have to start when they are young and have not formed these biases. Children are the same all over the world. They are open and trusting and ready to be taught. Without loving mentors they fall back into the prejudices of their parents. So we must reach out to them while they are young.

As I point out, the problem is not limited to South Sudan. There are women and children all over the world who need help to survive in our troubled times. I am a survivor. I provide the reader with my wisdom, the lessons I have learned of how to survive. I do not stop there. I want everyone to have a better and happier life. I want you to understand that all adversity can be overcome by the right frame of mind. No matter how bad it looks, it is not that bad. Never give up hope. Hope is the road to a better future.

If you apply the wisdom, knowledge, experience, skills, strategies, and techniques offered in this book to your life, then you will find this an inspirational memoir to achieving hope and courage which will help you in overcoming adversity in difficult times. I cannot solve every problem and I do not have every answer, but these are the survival techniques I used in my life.

I understand why you have not pursued all your dreams, goals, and visions. I know that you may be a single parent, working 2-3 jobs, going to night school, or struggling to get an education. I want you to know that it is okay and I believe in you. I want to be the shoulder that you can lean on during tough times. I want to be your friend. I want to help you overcome your challenges and be the person and resource that you look towards to overcome your challenges. Are you ready to expand your comfort zone and step into the new person that you are becoming? Are you ready to achieve your goals? If so…good, let's get started and make this journey together! Now is your time! Let's Go! I challenge you to take action. You cannot provide aid to any lost soul without taking charge. Every good thought must be followed by good action.

— Ayak Mithyang

1

BELONGING TO MY PARENTS

"We are apt to forget that children watch examples better than they listen to preaching."

— Roy L. Smith

My name is Ayak Mithyang and this is my life story. I have been through a lot in my life. My goal in writing this book is to be an inspiration to you and your life to help you overcome all of the struggles, obstacles and adversities that you face.

BEING IN A CIVIL WAR

The First Sudanese Civil War was ended by the Addis Ababa Agreement with the accords being incorporated in the Constitution of Sudan. This agreement united the regions of South Sudan under its own autonomous government. This resulted in Moslem Sudan being separated from African South Sudan. On 16 May, 1983, Dr. John Garang joined an army mutiny he had been sent to put down, and Salva Kiir Mayardit and other Southern leaders joined the Sudan People's Liberation Army (SPLA) to form the rebel Sudan People's Liberation Movement (SPLM). Then, on 5 June

1983 Sudan President Gaafar Nimeiry declared all Sudan an Islamic state under Shari'a law, including the non-Islamic southern region. The Southern Sudan Autonomous Region was abolished and the Addis Ababa Accords were nullified.

Sudan and South Sudan had suffered from numerous internal conflicts over political, ethnic, and religious issues since it received independence from British rule. The driving force behind this war has been portrayed as an ideological conflict between Islam and African customs, however the main driving force is over who controls the oil deposits in South Sudan -- less a war of principle and more a war of greed.

This conflict rapidly escalated into the Second Civil War. Dr. Garang De Mabior had advanced military knowledge and experience from both the United States and Sudan, and Kiir served as his deputy. Although portrayed as a military conflict between Sudan and the Sudan People's Liberation Army, the conflict degenerated into conflicts between the native tribes and both armies, as both armies were pressing brutal Islamic Shari'a law.

Thousands of South Sudanese people were murdered, tortured and raped. The conflict has killed two million people. War, famine and disease displaced more than four million people from South Sudan. The civilian death toll is the highest of any war since World War II and the human rights violations, including slavery and mass murder, rival the Holocaust and the Cherokee Trail of Tears.

Here begins my story.

COMING IN THE NIGHT

I was born January 1st 1984 in Abyei, South Sudan during the war. The leaders of South Sudan lived in Khartoum. They were Moslem. They sell and kill and rape. No one was safe.

They come in the night. They come with loud orders and mean shoving. They come looking for me. Why do they want me. I haven't done anything. I am just a girl. Someone says, "That is why they want you! Because you are a girl!" They take the girls and use them up. Then they leave them in the street. These girls can't work because they are girls. They can't work so they have no money to buy food. They have their babies there on the street. They huddle with their babies crying because they have nothing to feed them. What can you do? These poor girls have no hope.

They always attacked us in the dark. When the Muslims came to the village to attack people from my village it was always at night. And when they took my father away and killed him it was at night. And when they killed my mother it was at night. I think that's good reason to name my book after these attacks. Yes. I think I'm going to name the book: *They Attack Us In The Dark*, because that is what they did. Because when they attacked us, it was always in the dark. Like monsters hiding in the dark. And when they took my dad it was in the dark and in the night.

So how did this happen?

I was born to an ordinary family of the Dinka people. My name was given me as Ayak Deng Madut Mithyang. Mithyang is my father's grandfather's name. Madut is my grandfather's name. Deng is my father's name. I was given my name, Hayat Deng by the Moslems in order to attend school because that was what was going on at that time. In Dinka, "Ayak" means "rain stopped, beautiful but dry and no food." That was the time I was born in. When I was born the Dinka were suffering from a long drought and we had no food. My father's name was "Deng" meaning "rain" because that was what it was like the time he was born. That is how Dinka are named.

My dad worked away from home and I did not see much of him. My family was Dinka and I was Dinka. My tribe did not have much. We did not have schools or doctors. The children played pretty much as they pleased, doing whatever babies do.

Then one night in the dark when I was less than two years old, there were shouts and commands and they took my dad. Big men came in my house with flashing lights in the dark. They were yelling at my mother and my father. That was when they took him. He hardly had a chance to look back. I never saw him again.

My mother was left with us children and no man to support our family.

Women had a very hard time trying to support a family in South Sudan. When my mother was looking for a job they had slaves and the only work she could find was housekeeping, midwifing and being a servant. So she did that. So you see what my mother went through. But this is what you have to do to live and support your children.

I want to make one thing clear about my mother. My mother worked hard cleaning houses and she was always busy as a midwife. We didn't have much money, but she worked hard for what we had.

There were so many women and young girls on the street with their babies. They could not work. Their babies were always crying because they were hungry and the street girls had no food to give them and could not work to get money to buy food. That is how bad it was.

Moslems believe in Jesus but they believe he was a teacher, not the son of God. So Moslems do not believe in the Christian Sacrament, baptism or the manifestations of the spirit. As a result there is an uneasy tension between the Moslem community and the non-Moslem Dinka community. In Sudan, both north and South, the government is Moslem and the leaders of both nations assume that everyone is obligated to obey strict Moslem law. It is as though they assume you are Moslem. You can be a Christian or a Dinka or a member of another tribe and the government does not accept that you are different. It is quite a challenge. They assume you are a bad Moslem -- even when you are not really a Moslem at all. It is very bad if you are Dinka practicing your tribal beliefs. It is even worse if you are a girl. You have no rights. Sometimes it means losing your life.

I do not remember much of this time. When I was one year old, I was just a baby.

FLEEING TO NORTH SUDAN

So this is what my mother faced. For a female to get a job in South Sudan, it's like a person killing twenty elephants by their own hands; bare-handed, not with any weapon; that's how hard it is for a female in South Sudan to get a job.

My mother, brothers, sister, and I went to North Sudan for safety in 1985, as the war was in South Sudan. My father was not able to come with us because he was forced to stay by the Omar government. I do not know what he was doing. I do know that my mother was afraid for him. He was Dinka and some of the Dinka were at war with the government in Khartoum. The government seemed to think that my father was a leader of the Dinka people.

The Dinka had formed The Sudan People's Liberation Army in 1983 to protect the Dinka from the South Sudan government headquartered in Khartoum. They would continue to fight this Second Civil War for 21 years and they took my father during the second year of this fight. Later, after the soldiers became numb to the constant fighting, all they would think about was survival and they would become as brutal as the government forces. But in the early days of the war, The Sudan People's Liberation Army, was purely humanitarian, trying to protect the Dinka people.

Arriving in North Sudan, we settled in Omdurman where my mother started working. She struggled to try to provide a living for us. She couldn't afford to put us in school, and we could only have one meal a day.

My mother started working in North Sudan as a midwife and cleaning houses to provide for me and my siblings. She managed under terrible conditions for fourteen years, until 1998. North Sudan was completely run by Moslems and Dinka women did not receive very much respect.

I learned Arabic and learned how to fit in with the Moslem community. When I started school in Omdurman I had to have a Moslem name so I was called pronounced "Hayet Deng." This does not translate very well. "Hayet" means *light* or *teacher* in Arabic. The Arabic sounds a little like my name but is not my name.

I attended the mosque while I attended school. I thought it was called Jamic Mosque. I was also in the Nilian Mosque.

My Mother. She was a very strong and faithful woman. She had tremendous faith, and provided perfect examples to us children. She gave us as much as she could, and taught us everything a child should be taught by their mother.

When I was a child I followed the old religion and spoke the Dinka language. When I fled to North Sudan with my life I learned to speak Arabic and learned the Moslem ways. When I immigrated to the United States I learned English, sort of, as I am still learning how to write in English. Sometimes I cannot read what I have written.

The school was a Moslem school and I was taught Arabic and Islamic teachings. We spoke Arabic in school and had to live under Moslem rules. While in Sudan the only religion I knew was Islam. This helped me as I grew up because I was able to talk with the Moslems as one of them. Although

Moslems do not treat women with respect, they treat Moslem women better than Dinka women.

I was raised in a small poor home. We didn't have enough to eat, but mother, she was feeding us with love all the time. That love, that's the most beautiful thing that she brought along with us.

Every day we made tea in the morning. That was our breakfast. Then our mother would go to work and we would go to school. Then, me and my siblings, we would come home and do our homework. After that we would clean our house and ourselves. Then we waited for our mother. She would arrive around 6:00 pm. As soon as she arrived we would make a campfire so we could cook our dinner together. Then we would eat together from our one plate. The reason why we waited so late to eat was that if we ate at lunch we wouldn't have enough food to eat dinner. So dinner was the only meal we had. Also, it is hard to sleep on an empty stomach.

Most of the time we didn't have a roof over our heads. A lot of times we would lie down and look at the stars and watch the moon.

My mother was struggling trying to provide a living for us. She had so little that she couldn't afford to put us in school. So, we barely survived. We could only have one meal a day and sometimes we went to sleep with no meal. She provided as much as she could for us.

No matter how hard times got, mother was always gentle and loving. My mother was always smiling. We never saw her stressed out.

WAITING TO HEAR FROM MY FATHER

When I was fourteen my mother and sister went back to South Sudan in the January 1998 to see my father because he was still not able to come north to see his family. When my mother went back to South Sudan she couldn't take me. She had to leave me behind because they come in the night. Those Moslem men come in the night to take away the girls and the men. So my mama couldn't take me with her because it was too dangerous in South Sudan.

On April 8th 1998 my father and about a hundred men were captured by the Northern Army of the Omar Bashir Government and taken away by force in front of my mother and sister. Three days later a man escaped back to the village and told my mother that he saw about twenty men get their necks cut through but did not see my father get killed. We have been waiting since then, but we never saw our father again.

A couple of months later my mother and sister came back to North Sudan where I had been left with my three older brothers and my aunt. My mother explained to us that our father was taken away. She said our father had been taken away on April 8 and never made it back.

My mother continued working as a midwife and cleaning woman. My older brothers started working as mechanics to help my mom.

EXERCISES

1. Where were you born? What was the economic social and political environment at the time of your birth?

_____

_____

_____

_____

_____

2. Consider your own life. Write below your mission in life. How do you want to love and serve the world.

_____

_____

_____

_____

_____

AYAK'S WISDOM

1. How do you go from stressed to feeling blessed?

   Life is not just a bump in your path. You can't go over it, you can't go around it, so you can only go through it. You have to stop avoiding it. You just got to go through this. If you don't fight against what God has placed in your life you will find your road much smoother. God helps you if you are willing to listen to Him with love in your heart.

2. Why do you say you don't want to think about your problems?

   When the engine light is on, it doesn't go away because you ignore it. We have to recognize the problem to fix the problem.

3. How do you survive when life is hard?

   To move forward refugees must realize that motherlands have been replaced with other lands and you have been punished by war. I believe that peace is more than just diamonds and money. When things are bigger than you, the peace you will find will be in your own heart.

4. How do you protect children from being born in terrible circumstances?

   I'm sharing this with complex emotions and spirit, but a clear mind. As a child of God, and as a citizen of his kingdom, I am standing up for children who have not yet lived in the world. I want to make a world where children can create friendship across the world. Join me and help protect the children of the world.

2

LIVING IN EGYPT

"Everything you ever wanted is on the other side of fear."

— Anonymous

GOING TO EGYPT

When I was eighteen, in 2002, I went to Egypt and started working. My mother went back to South Sudan with my three brothers.

Since we both live in the same house we both need clean clothes, a clean house, and clean dishes. Helping out around the house does not make you less of a man. It is a partnership. When a woman causes problems hurting others, or their partner she is crying for love. She is trying to wake up from the hurt. She is just crying for love and trying to be heard.

If you go up there where she is hurting and give her the understanding she is crying for, if you give it all the way, you kill imagination. She imagined everything would be healed if you understood and gave her the love understanding she wanted. But imagination is not reality. So a woman gets what she wants and is not happy. The harder it is when they get it; the better they are treated when they get it.

GETTING MARRIED

When I turned nineteen, while I was still in Egypt, I got married. It is a Dinka custom to keep your last name when you marry because it honors your father and ancestors. My father would be upset if I changed my name because he is king over me. He is master of his daughter. My father raised me, he did everything he could, so my father tells my husband I raised this girl and you are not going to take her away from me. It's like milking a cow, you don't take the cow with you. You just take the milk and leave the cow.

In South Sudan most of the girls don't have choices. Coming from Sudan to Egypt I still felt I had no choices. The people I came to in Egypt told me I should marry this man. I didn't know him. I never saw him before. He was introduced to me by his cousins and they convinced me to marry him. They made it seem like I wouldn't have a life if I didn't marry him. They said, "You'll never find another husband." They made it sound like it was my only choice. I would never find anyone else who would marry me. I was just a poor girl who spoke tribal African. I was just an orphan and I had no future. Well, I couldn't argue with them. I was at their mercy so I went ahead and married him. I married him without a choice. When they talked to me, my hope was taken away. They made me 99% convinced that if I didn't marry him then, I would stay single the rest of my life. I was a young girl so I went ahead and believed them. They shook my faith. They scared me.That was on May 31, 2002. I got married and continued working. But you never know how things will turn out. Today I'm blessed with two beautiful smart children and I'm grateful for that. And that being said, I was a good wife and a good mother and a friend and a good cook. I kept the house clean and I kept everyone fed.

I always worked hard in my life. I did my best to always complete my work and I always made sure I did as good a job as I could. My husband relied on me to make a good wage because I was working for both of us. For a long time we had a happy home.

Some men don't grow up. He wants me to treat him like a boy, but I refused. He is a grown man who knows how to pull his own pants down. I have a boy already in the house and I am trying to raise him to be a man. One morning he woke me up completely changed. He became aggressive and physical. The day he put his hand on me, that day everything died inside me. And I wasn't in love anyway so it was easy to see him as a stranger. So now you are going to view me badly because I left my husband, but I was scared for my children. Most women have a good man. I didn't. Like a fish when the fish is full, it is fine, but it will jump out of the water at the first sign of trouble. Before that morning I didn't know what to look for. From that experience I learned the difference between a green light and red light. When I saw the green light I stepped on the gas.So, I didn't know my kids father before I married him and I didn't know him that morning. So then I took my kids and left. I provided everything we needed. I worked for a time and made sure that they had all they needed. Knowing my kids are safe it feels good sitting in the dark.

LOVING SOMEONE

If you ever fall in love, fall in love with someone who loves you the way you smile. Fall in love with someone who kisses you in public and is proud to show you off to anyone they know. Don't let a man fool you or change you. You need a man in your life that knows the word of God and holds you accountable and treats you like a blessing.

Be yourself; don't try to be somebody else; obey God; and love because you're brand new heart says it, not because somebody told you to do so.

- Rule number one: Be you.
- Rule number two: Think twice before making a decision.
- Rule number three: Make your decisions on your own.
- Rule number four: Don't tell anybody what you are going to do until you finish what you were going to do.

GROWING A RELATIONSHIP

Growing a relationship is like growing hair. If you use a wrong product it will damage your hair.On relationships between two people on opposite sides of the world: If you try approaching a relationship around the world, it will damage everything in the relationship, and will stop everything from growing further.Sometimes people want to change you into someone you are not. You have to accept people as they are. The only way people change is when they sincerely want to improve themselves. You can't do it for them. You can't force ice into a Jello mold. You can't put a leash on fire.Don't let anyone build you. You're not a house. When you allow them to build you like a house they will have the same power to break you down when they're ready to remodel their house or to make a different style of the house. You can't let things get to you. You can't let people control how you feel. Things happen. When things happen you just have to accept it and move on. The past is the past. Never let the past control your future. You just have to let disturbing things slide. Forgive and forget. Never let anyone disturb your peace while they're in the way with somebody else.

EXERCISES

1. If you were a refugee escaping from a militaristic government, what would you fear most?

____

____

____

____

____

2. What are your feelings regarding refugees finding themselves sheltered under a foreign government whose representatives speak a different language and have different customs? Are your feelings different when considering the adult refugees and the children refugees?

____

____

____

____

____

AYAK'S WISDOM

1. Why do you obsess over someone who does not want you?

   You can't turn water to water, but you can turn water to ice. Sometimes we hold onto and cry over someone that is not for us because we do not want to go through the hardships alone. When your heart is hard as ice you cannot feel love. You want someone to love you, you have to be willing to flow like water and accept the love that is given to you.

2. Why do you think so much about money that you don't have?

   You can be short a couple hundred dollars and you can still make it. But when we come up short with God, that's when we feel lost, confused, and lonely.

3. What do you do when there are problems in your marriage?

   Some people are killing you slowly. Watch for those people. Just because they're quiet doesn't mean they like you. Ask yourself, have you seen a snake?

   It is not your fault when your marriage doesn't work. It is not your spouse's fault either. Do not blame people when you cannot get along with someone. Not everyone likes vanilla pudding. Some people simply are not suited for each other. I am not saying all marriages are bad. Some are wonderful. But sometimes trying to preserve a bad marriage simply will not work. All you need to provide to your marriage is lots of love and hard work. Marriage is not easy.

3

COMING TO AMERICA

"We are a nation of immigrants. We are the children and grandchildren and great-grandchildren of the ones who wanted a better life, the driven ones, the ones who woke up at night hearing that voice telling them that life in that place called America could be better."

— Mitt Romney

COMING TO AMERICA

I immigrated to America!

September 9, 2004, I came as a refugee to America.

I am really grateful to have had the opportunity to come to America. I want to help those children who lived the same life I lived in Africa by providing them education and health by building schools and health care centers throughout South Sudan. I want these kids to have an opportunity where they can learn and make friends across the world. With the wonderful help provided by others, you can make a difference in the world. To me, coming to America meant I could make a difference.

In America I could make a decent living. I have to give a big thanks to America to opening a door for others.

I arrived in the United States as a refugee. I worked hard and can now share what I have with those I left behind. I am truly grateful to have this opportunity to help the children of South Sudan, who are living the same life I lived before. I want to help provide education and health, by building schools and health care centers throughout South Sudan where kids can learn and make friends across the world. I had big dreams when I came to America.

I came straight to California and I stayed with my sister.

First thing, when we came to America, I went to the store and I bought a dog cereal. I didn't know that it was a dog food. So when I was pregnant with my son I ate it. It made me sick and I was puking for a long time. So I told my sister, "American foods don't taste good like what I was told." My sister said, "You can try different foods. Which one was you eating?" And I showed her. Everyone was laughing for seven days. She said, "This is not a human food. This is animal food." I was like "What the heck?"In 2005 I had my first child. My son was born in San Diego, CA. His name is Kout Dau.

EXERCISES

1. Have you ever married or considered getting married? List any special requirements that you think your spouse should have.

_____

_____

_____

_____

_____

2. Do you think you are submissive or demanding? List two or three ways you are submissive and two or three ways you are demanding.

_____

_____

_____

_____

_____

3. Consider your answers in question two above, how are you being unrealistic?

_____

_____

_____

_____

_____

AYAK'S WISDOM

1. Why do you complain about your life?

   I love the way God raises me up, how he lifts me up, and turns me around to become a beautiful woman and a mom, loving, responsible, confident, forgiving, and caring. I love how God blesses me. If you want to be blessed in your life you have to be thankful for the blessings that you have. If you acknowledge all the blessings that you have you will not complain.

2. Why do you think things were better in your past?

   Stop talking too much about the best things in your past. Your past should be one, two, and three. That's it. If he or she keeps asking about your past she or he is not the right person for you -- keep moving. He or she is looking for something to use against you when things are going down, that's why the person keep asking you about your past so many times. Your past is dead and buried; Even if it was perfect you want to leave it behind anyway. Oh yeah.

3. Why are you pretending you are someone you are not?

   Building a fake relationship is like building a fake resume. I know what a fake resume looks like. I know what it is when they say, "Oh I've been working there for three to five years but I don't remember the phone number, supervisor, address, or name of the company."

4. Should I submit to someone who abuses me?

   Men you should always treat a woman with respect and dignity. Women give birth to presidents, doctors, teachers -- you can name it. Spouses should never abuse each other. You have to support each other. Marriage is a partnership.

5. Is it unkind to avoid people who complain and are negative about everything?

   Collect your garbage and make sure you take it to the landfill do not dump it on me.

4

LIFE OF AN AFRICAN WOMAN

"Ethnicity should enrich us; it should make us a unique people in our diversity and not be used to divide us."

— Ellen Johnson Sirleaf

DESERTING YOUR WIFE

In 2006 we moved to Seattle, Washington. I was twenty-two.

Most African men, when a woman has their first child they don't see her as attractive anymore. They look down on her, especially when the man is the one who is the provider. What they don't appreciate is when a woman stays home with her kids. Children, they are a full time job. The only difference between a 7-5 job and a mother's work at home taking care of the children is that one gets paid and the other doesn't. So every mother deserves a break.

Those men just move on to the next women. And that is what my husband did. I ask these men: What kind of legacy do you want to leave behind? Do you want your children to grow up without a father? They don't say yes or no. They feel guilty so they just leave. Their children grow up without a father and when they are grown they don't know how fathers should act. So, they do the same thing their fathers did.

It needs to stop here so the next generation doesn't fall into the same box. There's already been enough damage. Many generations have been affected by this same act.

BEING A MOTHER

If that man paid attention to what's in front of him he would realize he already has the most beautiful woman. Beauty is not in novelty. You do not appreciate and love your mother because she was young. When your mother got old would you replace her with a younger woman? That is silly. Your mother is always beautiful. Your wife is always beautiful. Your husband is always handsome.

ENSLAVING OTHERS

A slave was not named by God; just some people came together and thought they were doing the right thing. They used their own brain and power which anyone could do, including black people, because god created everybody the same. He didn't say that black and white can't be together in the same place or they can't eat at the same table or drink the same water. At the end of the day everybody came together again because it wasn't God's plan to give people power to enslave others. Anyone could have done this too, and that's why everything has a season. There is a season for bad and for good; a season for crying and for laughing; and that's just part of life.

It's hard enough to control the rain, so you simply can't control other people's thinking. What matters the most is that God gave us all free choice. You should not worry about what others are thinking because you do enough damage on your own.

BLAMING OTHERS

Don't blame everything on others. Blaming others is why most of South Sudanese and black fathers walk away from their children. The moment you walk out that door, the moment you hurt the child's life, you are responsible. Your child depends on her or his mother and father. You are man enough to lay down with her and make them children, then be man enough to take full responsibility. Don't blame your children. They didn't ask to be here. You both decided to bring them into this world, so you must take care of them. A child should not wake up in the morning and not have a roof over their head. most black kids wake up in the morning and their father is not there. The excuse for black people is this: The color! Just because you are black doesn't mean you can't take responsibility for your own children. When a man walks away he's not walking away from the woman, he's walking away from his own children. Just because both of us, husband and wife, can't get it together that doesn't include the children.

It is bad for a child waking up every morning without their father. Most of African or Black fathers walk away from their children's lives. The moment you walk out that door, the moment you hurt that child's life remember that child depends on her or his mother and father. You are man enough to make a child, be man enough to fulfill your responsibility. The child did not ask to be here, we both decided to bring a child into this world, so we must together provide what the child should have in their life. The child should not wake up in the morning without food on the table and a roof over their head. Most black kids wake up in the morning with no dreams because nobody is supporting them.

Irresponsibility -- That's the problem with us as people. When some people try to do good, other people get jealous of them. They want to destroy their life so everybody can live in the same old box. That is very wrong. If you can't get your thing together let others be.

All society is going off in half-brained ways; nobody is going in a fully wise direction. Rich and poor are the same: Rich people are worried about their money and lives. Poor people are worried about how to pay their bills. Being positive and confident can help you achieve your dreams. You need to start using your brain to reach your goals and dreams. Dreams are hard to achieve but don't let anyone let you down.

Fathers start being around your children. The world has had enough of children waking up every morning without their father. That's what's causing a lot of children growing up with a disability. Its better when your parents are dead. It's a different understanding than when your parents are alive, but refuse to take care of their own children.

BEING ON WELFARE

Most black men do not want to work and that's been going on from generation to generation. That's not stopping. But it's got to stop right here, right now. Why should our children be on welfare all the time? Irresponsible! That's the problem with black people. That is why you are on food stamps all the time.

Life can be tough sometimes and that's why it is important to have money. A lot of families I have talked to, many of their children are on aid. When I asked some parents they say that their children are too hyper. That is not the case. The case is that a lot of them want to just stay home so they have reason to get money from the government. That is very wrong. They are putting their kid's life on fire. It breaks my heart when children should be exploring the world but are stuck on medication. That's a shame. I don't know how their heart allows them to do that. The medication should be used as needed, not just to use it to get what you want to get, because when a child gets addicted to medication it is just like alcohol. You feel like you are missing something. It is not smart thinking at all. You need to take this more seriously because a lot of children are losing their life because of that. Simple -- If you can't take care of them don't make them. Sincerely -- Make the effort to stop.

There is nothing like your hard earned money. Even if you are making 5$ an hour, people will respect you. I know the whole world is going wrong, but that does not mean that is how life should be. You could make a difference in the world if you used your brains wisely.

BEING POLITE

One day I went to a restaurant with a homeless man. We sat for about 10 minutes and nobody said anything to us. The waitress kept staring at us so I got up and walked to her. I said, "Excuse me? Can we get the menu please?" She gave me a menu, but she did not say anything, she just handed it to me. I walked up to her again to show her what we wanted to order. She asked me if it was okay if I could pay first. I said sure and I gave her my credit card. She charged the meal and gave me back my credit card with a receipt. Fifteen minutes later we got our order and she asked us, "Is there anything else I can get for you guys?" I said, "No, mam. Thank you very much." Five minutes later she walked back up to us again and asked if everything was good so far. We both responded back to her, "Yes, mam. Everything is good." After we were done eating I left 20 dollars on the table as a tip. On our way out she came behind us and said, "Thank you so much guys. Have a wonderful evening." I told her, "You do the same mam. Thanks again." Sometimes you have to treat people in their way of thinking. Just because she was acting unprofessional, it doesn't mean I can do the same thing that she did. You don't want people to change your mood 0r make you change the way you live your life. I'm sure that night she went home and thought about how she treats people, assuming she has a good heart.

BEING PREJUDICED

Now, I took this homeless man across the street to VONS to get some groceries for him. The manager asked him to leave the store "right now." I turned around and told her that we were going to shop and leave. She responded back to me and said, "If he doesn't leave right now, I will call the cops on him." I told her, "If it is going to solve the problem then go ahead." You have to treat other people the way you want to be treated because things happen for a reason. You laugh today you cry tomorrow. Nobody knows what happens tomorrow. You might need the person that you treated badly. That's why you need to be careful of how you look at other people. Don't look down at people.

You don't get what you want all the time because that's part of life. Sometimes you don't eat all the lettuce in your salad, because some leaves are good and some bad. There's no perfect life. Life will never be perfect, but you can make the way just about okay. Nobody has a perfect life on this world. No one knows the destination of any person's life. The only one who has control of your life plan is God. You don't always get what you want all the time. You don't know why, other than it's because it's a part of life.

Sometimes a person you help will help you one day. Even if they don't, a good deed blesses the world when you pay it forward.

SPREADING NEGATIVITY

Life will never be perfect, but you can just make the way be okay. When somebody is trying to do good, other people get jealous of them. They want to destroy **your** life so everybody can live in the same box. That is very wrong. If you can't get your things together then let other people be. Just let them be. The only way to ignore negative people is to let them bark like a dog.

If you can't get your own things together, then let other's things be. The only way to ignore wrong folks is to let them bark like dogs while you move forward.

Never hate jealous people. They are jealous because they think you are better than them. If a person laughs at you all the time he or she may need some deep help. Negative people are not happy for you. When you achieve something good in your life, they don't like you because their life is full of drama and they want to dig you into their drama. They want to keep you under their control and in fear. People start having fear and start creating problems with you when they can't reach your level. When they can't show the love you show; when they can't have you in their control; when they can't copy your life style; that is when people start having fear. That is when they create problems with you.

Never fixate on other people's lifestyle. You are strong. Use your strength to change yourself instead of changing other people. Focus on yourself and learn how to let go. When you are able to drop the things you don't need; when you stop providing negative things to people; when you stop comparing your life with others; when you find yourself; when you prove people's negative thinking wrong; then you can treat other people the way you want to be treated.

I have one lady who used to come to my daycare and every time she came, she just talked negative all the time and all her talks are racist. She kept telling me, "You're not going to achieve any dreams while you're in this country because you are coming from a different country and nobody wants you to go up." I told her, "Sorry, I don't believe in that because there is no perfect country. That's why I'm here in America. If my country were perfect I wouldn't have come here to America, but America is better than where I was."

Being negative is not going to let you go higher, but being positive can help you achieve your dreams. "I know what I want." I told her, "You need to teach your kids the right things so they don't feel the same way you're feeling. It's a bad feeling. How long are you going to feel that way? You have to move on. You need to start using your brain in a smart way to reach your goals and dreams. Your thinking is affecting society. Let's try to make a difference in society instead of pulling back. It's good to have plans. Have plans, all the time. But, don't let people bring you down. Never change your dreams because of somebody else."

You want to let others know what love is. You need to show them what love is. When people hurt you, just say, "Thank you for giving me a chance to learn about you." Never say any more. Never tell anyone more about you. Never tell anyone the pains that hurt the most because they will just use that knowledge against you to hurt you more. Just show them your smile.

Life is too short to waste on negative people.

RESPECTING DREAMS

Let's not rely on things. Let's rely on God more. He's the only one who plans things for us. Respect other's cultures. God knows dream plans are hard to follow for human beings, but don't let anyone take those dreams away from you. Have you ever tried to find the words but they don't come out right? Have you ever done anything to make others understand? Or, do you just feed the devil your secret? Your enemies are your devil. If you just keep trying, finally the devil will give up and get out of your way.

God has sent you all you need. He opens doors for you, but time after time you shut those doors he opened. You need to learn how to keep them open by keeping your mouth closed.

I had a dream while I was in Egypt that I could make a difference if I came to America. By hard work, a lot of prayer, and a little faith, dreams can come true.

SURVIVING

After all these troubles I pulled myself together and said to myself, I am a survivor. I will get through this. My life will be a success because I will make it a success. How will I do this? I will do this by looking at all the good things God has given me. I will do this because I have a beautiful son.

EXERCISES

1. We are not all African women but we are all human. Have you ever had a close friend or spouse? Write below the best thing you ever did to respect that person.

____

____

____

____

____

2. Have you ever felt you were struggling through a difficult time? Possibly you found the COVID pandemic a struggle for you. Write below the one lesson mentioned above that would be of particular help to you in such a struggle.

____

____

____

____

____

AYAK'S WISDOM

1. How should I treat my wife?

   Just like grass requires water to keep it green and beautiful, women require love, respect, energy, compliments, trust, and honesty to keep them beautiful.

2. How should I treat my children?

   Be a strong woman so your daughter knows how to be one and your son knows how to pick one.

3. How should I treat my husband?

   Just like husbands should treat wives, wives should treat their husbands with love, respect, energy, compliments, trust, and honesty to keep their thoughts from wandering.

5
PARENTING

"It is not what you do for your children, but what you have taught them to do for themselves that will make them successful human beings."

— Anonymous

BEING A PARENT

In 2007 my daughter was born in Washington. I may get it fixed someday but it is a very complicated thing to do. So now I have two beautiful children. To make it easier to work and care for my children I started working as a caregiver. Then, the father of my two kids started being abusive. We suffered both physical and emotional abuse.Parents are the ultimate role models for children. Every action and argument has an effect. If you want to help a child, sincerely go to both parents in the child's life and say, "You can plan life together." Raising a child is just like planting a tree. It takes many years and much strength. During those many years you have to water the tree so it doesn't die. That's a part of raising a child. Do your best by providing everything a child should have from their parents and leave the rest to God. You have to get up every morning and work hard. God doesn't bring everything to you while you are in bed doing nothing. You have to work for it.Children won't always follow your advice but they will follow your example. No other person or outside force has greater influence on a child than the parent. Our children are sponges. They soak up everything.So it's best to ask..... Is what you do or say the way you want your children to be? If not then lets change that so the next generation doesn't fall into the same example.In life, success with your children depends on who you chose to keep your family safe and healthy. People in your house also affect your children. So be careful who is influencing your children. Some people come into your life for a season and some come for a lifetime. You need to recognize which is which so you don't hurt your loved ones.If I could go back again I would choose the same kids. I have, but with a different father than they have now. My kids are my kids and they are a blessing in my life. They changed my life. They changed the way I used to think. They are smart kids -- Full of joy, love, respect, dignity, and faith.How do I support my own children? I feel the most important influence in their life that I can give them is showing them what a strong woman does. I hold them close and love them. I never criticize them or express any negativity around them. All my influence is positive. I want to uplift them. We go to church together and worship together. We share everything and support each other. I do not believe in punishment because my children never do anything that deserves punishment. No child deserves to be belittled or hurt. You must support your children in everything they do the best you can. They understand when I am working and help as best they can. When you allow children to bloom like beautiful flowers they will bloom. Children are sponges and they will soak up everything you do. They have very long memories and will not forget any harsh word they hear. At the same time they are eager to do good and anxious to please their parents. Working with hundreds of children I have never met a bad child.

PARENTING RULES

These are the rules I follow both in caring for my own children and caring for the children of people who bring their children to my Daycare Center or the children I help through Ayak's Helping Hands.

1. Raising children is a sacred duty assigned to families by God. If you remember that your children are God's children you will know that they are special and wonderful.
2. Parents, love your children. You should always be proud of your children no matter what they do. You must support them for them to know that they are loved.
3. Set an example of righteous living. This means living the life God wants you to lead. For my family this means living lives of light and truth and following the gospel teachings.

4. Provide for your children's physical needs. They need food, shelter, health care, exercise and friends.
5. Provide for your children's spiritual needs. The best way to do this is to set a good example of how you want them to be. If you want them to be one way and you set a bad example don't be surprised when you mess them up. You need to show love to your family to teach your children what love is all about. If you want your children to obey God you need to observe the commandments of God and to be a law-abiding citizen yourself. You need to teach them how to worship Heavenly Father and how to gain a testimony of true things.
6. Provide your children with a good education. They need a good education to lead good productive lives. They need a good education to get good jobs. Parents teach their children when the family is together for meals and while working and playing together.

If you do this right your children will be healthy and happy. When your home is filled with the spirit of love and kindness and you are teaching your children the principles that Jesus taught you can have great joy in your family. If you have a strong, loving, happy home your children will grow up strong and be able to lead righteous, happy, and productive lives.

Always be positive. Always smile. Always be gentle.

EXERCISES

1. Have you ever been responsible for a child? List below any thoughts about how you could have improved how you acted.

____

____

____

____

____

____

____

2. Consider your own feelings about children. Write below your goals for helping children in the future.

____

____

____

____

____

____

AYAK'S WISDOM

1. I have trouble when every day is the same struggle. How do you keep it up?

   Keep close whatever tools you grabbed to save you when you were falling down. You are the one responsible for your life and may need those tools again.

You are not alone. You have God listening to you all the time. If you need His help He will help you, but you have to ask in faith.

Don't leave the world with nothing. Leave the world with an example behind you. When you feel so down and tired, you keep saying "l don't want to be here alone anymore." Well, you are not alone. You have the Lord. The jealous lord, he will never let anyone put you down. You may sometimes say, "It's impossible." But, everything with God is possible if you are close to him and trust him. You can't let go of your dreams because somebody thinks you can't succeed.

Keep your soul, your mind, and your heart. Don't give up. Your day will come. It's just a matter of time.

2. What do I do when someone is mean to me and hurts me?

   Remember what hurt you today makes you strong tomorrow. If the problem is serious report it. Whatever you do, don't hold grudges and don't hurt someone else because you are hurt. Injuries heal. Grudges are festering wounds that damage the soul. So just forgive and forget.

FALLING OUT OF LOVE

"Accept what is, let go of what was, and have faith in what will be."

— Sonia Ricotti

DIVORCING MY HUSBAND

People say, about arranged marriages, that when you live with your spouse for a while you will fall in love with them. I am not sure I ever fell in love so much as I got used to being married. But even that was not to last.

He told me that my job was to fry the chicken and clean the house. He just lay down all day expecting me to fry the chicken but he does not like to work. I asked him, "Does the chicken walk home by himself'. Don't you think you should go to work so you can buy the chicken so I can fry it?" I was working ten hot shifts six days a week. I would come home and he's still sleeping on the couch. Kids have not eaten; diapers are not changed since I left home. Sam. I go straight to changing diapers, cook and feed the family, go give the kids a bath, dress them for bed. You pray with them and put them in bed. Then I go back to the kitchen and clean up. I finally go to bed at 12:31 in the morning. I wake up at 4 the next morning.

His job was lying down, sleeping all day, and trying to tell me what I can and cannot do.

Finally I got tired. I decided to leave because I deserve better than that. I work hard. I am a responsible mother with good talent. I am intelligent, smart, and hardworking.

And I was taught by a strong mother to take one step at a time and keep looking forward. In 2008 I got divorced.

Problems are like lifejackets. The problem that floats your life today isn't there to drown you, but to teach you how to swim out of the darkness. See?

When you give your soul to the wrong man and he abuses it, he breaks your heart into pieces. By the time you leave he has already done more than enough damage.

How much damage depends on how long you stay in the relationship.

So, women, stop making excuses for the man that doesn't deserve your heart. Stop saying "He's good *sometimes,* and respects me *sometimes.*" He needs to love, and respect you all the time. If he only loves you when he's at home, or only loves you on his day off when he's not working, then that's a red flag telling you that you need to keep moving. Be familiar with red flags. Get out when the light starts getting blurry. Don't wait until it gets so dark you can't see the way out. Make sure you do this before you get married to them. Remember: most men, when you get them in bed, even if they don't love you, they stay with you.

SURVIVING DIVORCE

We moved to downtown San Diego to a domestic violence shelter for 30 days. We moved from shelter to shelter. After 30 days we moved to a different shelter for 60 days. After 60 days we moved to our last shelter in Vista. We stayed there for about four months and they gave us our own apartment. Sometimes it takes strength, faith, and confidence. I started working at Vons and stayed there for nine months.

When I was moving from shelter to shelter with my kids, I told them that it was just a temporary life: God has a plan for us I don't know where, how, or when, but I know the door will open soon because when one door closes, another one opens, and a strong woman always works hard and organizes her life with a tear in her eye.

The only power you can use is the power of prayer. Heavenly father is the only one who has plans for me and nobody else.

It takes only minutes to fall in love but it takes years to get out of abuse.

I started a daycare business and quit Vons. My landlord told me that if I closed down my daycare, then he would let me stay and I said, "Heck no!" I was not going to give up my kid's future. God has a plan for me. No one can push my head down. I kept going. Everything with God is possible. You can't let your dreams go just because somebody else thinks you should. No one is in charge of your life or your happiness. You can only trust yourself with your own life. Spread positivity. Take two to ten minutes a day to make someone smile.

I moved to a different house to continue my daycare business because I was not giving up.

Every day is a struggle. I ask God, "Help me walk through the world without getting my feelings hurt. Help me keep my heart pure and undivided. Protect me from my own careless thoughts and the devil. Lord help me to forever remember what a gift it is to sit with you like this."

Your fear controls the light. Whatever happens just let go. Don't let the devil win your heart. If it did, it would block the light of your future. Reliving fear and the past is not going to do you any good. Just let it go, leave it alone, because this is the moment for you to act. Why are you looking back?

RECOVERING

A single mother knows how to be strong even when she feels weak.

Now, one day you may look back and realize you changed your life for the best. Tell yourself, "I alone am strong enough to handle things that need to be handled." Don't lose yourself trying to please everyone else. While you are trying to find yourself by pleasing others, you are losing yourself.

Sometimes people hurt you and act like you hurt them. Stop and think, "Have you lost somebody but found yourself?" Sometimes you just have to stay silent because no words can explain your pain. Let them judge you, don't judge them. Your life is in front of you. It's up to you to make it right.

One thing money can't buy is love and confidence. You can say whatever you want but I love seeing people being happy and successful, because life is a journey not a competition. A strong woman is the one who wakes up every morning with a smile on her face.

Sometimes people seem angry. Sometimes these people are not angry, they just hurt. Some people are so quiet about their pain that they are tormented on the inside but are blank on the outside. I think, just a smile can change their mood.

There is a time in life when you feel that no matter what you do for some people it will return back to you bad. This is when it is important to remember that every little smile can touch someone's heart.

No one is born happy. If you take time to hurt people who hurt you, you won't have time to love people who love you. Have you ever done everything you could to help somebody and then found out how ungrateful they are? Sometimes you don't get it, so you do the same wrong things over, and over, and over again. You don't have to be that way. God turns us around. Sometimes you forget who God is. His greatness, his love, his caring, his excellence, and his power keep moving on. This freedom allows change and you will see these changes in the world you live in today. Today's world is totally different. God is not coming down here to correct or change anything that is already set in order. So anything God wants to do, or change, he is going to change through us. Sometimes you say, "Why are you in this trouble? It's because God trusts us with this trouble." Can you believe that or imagine that! Have you said a prayer for someone who has hurt you? Have you thanked them for the bad things they have done to you -- or forgiven them? Have you ever done everything you could to help somebody? Give it 'a go! If it seems difficult, take it one minute at a time. When you work in the moment time flies and all your work gets done. You look back and say, "How did I do so much?"

Thank everybody who has done something nice to you. Even when others do not return the kindness, know that Jesus did not give up just because things got unpleasant.

But it seems that you've been distracted by things that push us down and don't lift us up. You get distracted with selfishness and jealousy. It might seem that it is taking us a long time to do something. You are impatient. It's time for us to make up ground because you lost a lot of ground.

What do you do? This is not the time to give up. It's time to be resilient and focus. It's a test. It's time for us to come together as a people. It's time for us to act and make up time. This is not the time for us to quit.

EXERCISES

1. Who are the children in your life that you feel responsible for? Do not forget children who do not live with you.

____
____
____
____
____
____

2. Describe any event you have participated in that has benefitted the children of some community. How did this event benefit them? How did you go the extra mile for them.

____
____
____
____
____
____

AYAK'S WISDOM

1. How do you lead children to safety?

   African children live a racial life. Most of them are stuck where they are. They can't get out. I want to make pathways they can follow the path to get out.

2. Should you blame the government?

   I take this strong position for my motherlands. I have lived in four nations and I have always loved and respected my nation. Just because you get bad leaders does not make the nation bad. The nation is the people and I have always found that the people are good.

3. My friend wants me to promise something. Should I make a promise?

   Don't promise when you're angry and don't promise when you're happy. It takes 6 minutes to fall in love, but it takes a lot of energy and power to stand back on your feet when they hurt you. You can't hold on to something that doesn't want to stand up with you.

4. What is the best advice for a good life?

   Take ten to twenty minutes a day to smile, or make one to two other people smile.

5. How do I pick my friends and those I spend time with?

   Truly, if it's not right for you, just walk away before it's too late.

6. Why do you say you can't change people?

   It doesn't matter how hard you work trying to fix things that don't want to be fixed.

7. How do I control my feelings when I fall in love?

   Love is just like water. When it spills you can't pour it back into the cup.

8. Do people have a true love?

   Yes. There is someone out there God created just for you.

9. How doo you know you have found the right person?

   A good body will get old but a good man will always be a good man. The same applies to women. Wait until the infatuation has passed. When love is desperate there is no reasoning with it. True love lasts through all.

7

BEING CONVERTED

"Knowing that the gospel is true is the essence of a testimony. Consistently being true to the gospel is the essence of conversion."

— Elder David A. Bednar

BECOMING A SAINT

In 2009 some missionaries came to my door a couple times but I did not invite them in. I was going through domestic violence with the father of my two kids. I was praying to God to open doors for me to get out of the Darkness. And the missionaries kept coming back. They had not given up on me, so one day I let them in. They were missionaries of the Church of Jesus Christ of Latter-day Saints. They started talking about praying and how God can bless us through prayer and that touched my heart because that is what I was praying for.

And I started paying attention at that time and I asked them to come back again before they even asked me if they could. The second time they came we read scriptures. The third time I was ready to be baptized.

I was baptized on November 28th 2009.

After I was baptized I saw it -- a white bird. I started crying. People were wondering why I was crying. I told them I saw a white bird when I was baptized. My Bishop told me that it was an angel.

From a poor child in an African village -- to an arranged marriage as an Arabic teenager in Egypt -- to Sudanese refugee fleeing to America – to a white bird blessing me over the waters of baptism – it was a round-about way to end up in the church! It was the firm assurance that my father was alive in heaven and the positive attitude of the church towards death that got me through the next trouble in my life.

April 8, 2010 my mother was killed in South Sudan. Now I lost both parents. But I was old enough to understand. It did not hurt so much because my parents did not walk away from me. The war took them away from me. The one that hurts a lot is when your parents walk away from you.

You can't break down a woman who went through so much since she was a year old.

But the reason I did not break down and I kept winning and becoming stronger is because God and I, we had built a strong wall of protection around my soul that no one could break down.

The message is that you can't make others happy when you're not happy; you can't feed others when you're hungry; you can't love others when you can't love yourself; you can't bless others when you're not willing to receive your own blessings; you can't wash others hands when your hands are dirty. The bottom line is to do the best for you first.

Confidence is the most important thing that every person must have. You are who you are. Remember, people treat us based on our reactions and behavior. If you call yourselves smart you must act smart. Only one God created us, and we all die once. So, it's not based on color, nor is it because some people think they're better than others. If you believe in yourself then you don't need to worry about others. At the end of the day, white or black, we all have the same color of brain and blood. And again, we all die once.

I don't blame people sometimes when they say they are tired of other people. It took many, many, many, years of really good and hard work of brain and faith to establish and provide all the things that people try to abuse.

When someone cleans up your mess, you pray for them, thank them, and hope the best for them so God can bless you more positively. Sometimes confidence and faith make things easier and many people have trouble because they don't recognize this.

Play smart don't play rough. So don't kill yourself and others slowly by saying negative things because your own tongue can damage your own life too.

You can't let others make your decisions. Sometimes you even have to be careful with using others ideas to make your own decisions because some ideas are good and some are bad. Just as your fingers are not the same, so are human beings not the same either. All your fingers look like fingers and all people look like people, but you can't hold a cup pretending your little finger is your thumb. That's why there is history in the world. Our history helps us tell which ideas are good and which ones are bad.

On October 31, 2013, I moved from Washington back to California. I was twenty-nine years wiser. I told my bishop: "Today is a moving day. We are moving from Washington to California because my kid's father walked away from us. He refused to take responsibility as a father but now I have to take the position of both mother and father."

MY TESTIMONY

I want to leave the world with my testimony. The world we live in today is full of ants that are ready to eat every minute; so material things won't save us. You can have a house, a car, money. But when you are in times of trouble those things won't save you. What you need are good people in your life who can help you get back up. My church has people like that; good people.

The things we need to pray for are not just the material things. We need to pray for the good people in our life; those who pray for you when you're not able to pray for yourself. It is those people who can lift you up when you're not able to get up by yourself. It is those who think of you when you're not able to think for yourself. It is those who don't judge you. It is those who see things clearer when you're not able to see things clearly for yourself. Be grateful for every minute that God's breath is on you. I'm so grateful. Every morning I get up and go through my list of all those things I am grateful for.

EXERCISES

1. List the ways you have been blest in the last week.

____

____

____

____

____

2. Write the ways you have cheered up those around you during the last week.

____

____

____

____

____

AYAK'S WISDOM

1. I am not happy. What can I do?

   You need to begin with your health. You may need to talk to a doctor. If your health is fine, ask yourself what is making you unhappy? If it is another person then decide what needs to be done. Sometimes you can work out problems by changing yourself. Sometimes you can solve conflicts by talking it out. If the problem is with the world then pray and ask others for guidance. If the problem is yourself, then you may need counseling or you can try self-help courses. Faith in God is the ultimate answer. Members of my church are known the world over for being happier than most people. Why are they happy? They are happy because they have faith in God and a gospel that explains life and death. They are happy because they know where they will be after they die and they know they are loved. Also they know they can trust others in the church to be good people, not perfect, but good, who will help in times of trouble.

2. How do I make others happy?

Count your own blessings and share them with others. Sometimes being happy is contagious. The first place to start is sharing your love with someone else. Being kind to others helps lift their spirits. Be their friend. Talk to them. Find out what they like. Try to share experiences.

BUILDING A NEW LIFE

"In this fast-paced life, do we ever pause for moments of meditation—even thoughts of timeless truths? . . . Our Heavenly Father did not launch us on our eternal voyage without providing the means whereby we could receive from Him guidance to ensure our safe return. I speak of prayer. I speak too of the whisperings from that still, small voice; and I do not overlook the holy scriptures, which contain the word of the Lord and the words of the prophets—provided to us to help us successfully cross the finish line."

— President Thomas S. Monson,

MEETING THE BISHOP

In June 2014 I met a wonderful family with a perfect example for other families. Their names were Bishop Stephen Huyett and his beautiful wife Diane Huyett. They brought happiness to my heart and smiles to my face. They lifted me up when I needed it and cried with me when I cried and smiled with me when I smiled. They were with me through my tough seasons. Because of my lack of education I was not able to do paper work by myself. So my dear Bishop Stephen stepped up and helped me process the eviction papers. I don't know what I would do without this family. God sent them to me and my family for a reason. It isn't easy to find good people anywhere. When you find them you should be grateful and hope for the best for them too. Life is not perfect, but there's a way to make it easier without hurting others.

DAY CARE

I moved to California to start over again and today my heavenly father has blessed me with good people around me, support, and smart kids. I'm grateful for that. Things happen for a reason. I do not want anything to separate me from the Lord. I prayed, "Teach me how to choose only your way so my steps today will lead me close to you. Help me walk in the world so that hurt and fear does not fill my feelings. Help me to keep my heart pure and undivided. Protect me from my own careless thoughts and the devil. Words and actions can keep me from being distracted by other words. My desire and my thoughts are for how things should be. I recognize your love for me is not based on my performance. You love me, words and all. That's amazing. Lord help me to forever remember what a gift it is to sit with you like this."

At the end of 2013 we moved to an apartment.

In 2014 I started up my own daycare. I did it for one year. My landlord kept threatening to close my day care down or he would take me to court. The spirit warned him and I warned him to please stop. I was trying to get back on my feet and provide for my family. I was living with haters around the complex. Everybody signed a petition to get me out of the complex. After one year my landlord tried toevict me because I was running the day care. I went to the court and the case got dismissed.

Don't push my head back down. It is almost up. He continued pushing my head down and I told him, "I'm not going to give up. I will keep going because you don't know who you tried to hold down. Let me tell you who I am. I'm a child of god. I am His daughter and He is the only one who has a plan for me. Not you! Please stay away from me and my family." He took me to court anyway and the case for eviction was dismissed.No matter how bad things seem do not give up. I was with my two children and many families depended on my daycare service. I turned to my church and the good people there helped me find a new place to live and a place to run the daycare.

SETTING GOALS

You can help your children learn and develop by helping them set goals. It doesn't hurt to have goals of your own. Goals help you and your children grow into their eternal potential. And really, what can be better than that? It is easy to feel overwhelmed when asked to set goals. It can also be challenging to know how to begin and what to do.

You could set a bedtime so you don't stay up too late. Maybe you need to budget your money. Do you need to eat healthier or get more exercise? Maybe you need to learn a new skill or spend time improving an old skill. Do you want to avoid bad influences? Maybe you want to limit how much time is spent on social media or playing games. Maybe you want to do a random act of kindness each day for a month. You could decide to say "Hello" to someone new or befriend someone you know. You could participate in a service project to aid your community or help one child or one elderly person. There are many classes that you or your children could attend to improve their skills and teach them or allow them to participate in new and exciting things. Maybe you need to set a goal to save up money to allow yourself or your child to participate in a conference, a tour, or a trip. My favorite is to smile at everyone and get someone to smile back at you. You could join Ayak's Helping Hands.

Setting a goal is easy. All you have to do is choose something that would be good to do. It is usually helpful to write down this goal. Set a time to complete your goal and keep a notebook where you record your progress toward your goal. As you work toward your goal you may find that you need to do more things to complete your goal than you initially thought. Write down these new things and set goals to accomplish them. Never look at these new things to do as roadblocks. They are just bumps to get over. Always try to set reasonable times to accomplish your goals. You may have to talk with others or do research to set up these times. When you can't accomplish a goal in the time limit you set reevaluate your plan and set new goals. Never give up.

EXERCISES

1. Have you had a negative encounter or person in your life? Describe how you coped with that encounter or have forgiven that person.

____

____

____

____

____

2. Write below your best advice to someone who tells you of their own negative encounter.

____

____

____

____

____

AYAK'S WISDOM

1. People say I am argumentative. I can't just *agree* to *anything*.

   Don't be afraid to argue and disagree. Arguments are everywhere but it's not the argument that is important, its how you handle things. Don't let your past control your future.

2. I am afraid of many things. I am afraid of change.

Don't let your fear control the light. What ever happened just let it go. Don't let the devil win your heart so it cannot block the light of your future. Living the fear in the past is not going to do you any good. Just let it go, leave it alone because this moment is for you to live now. Why are you looking back?

FIGHTING BACK

"Adversity can come as a great storm to blow us off course and threaten to cast us against the rocks. But sometimes we are also in danger when everything appears to be safe— the winds soft and the waters smooth."

— Dieter F. Uchtdorf

WORKING HARD IS THE KEY

If you don't have enough money remembers this: With a lot of hard work and good education, anything is possible, even becoming president. That's what the American Dream is all about. Do not let anyone make you feel like you don't matter or like you don't have a place in the world. You have a right to exactly who you are. But I also want to be clear. This right isn't just handed to you. This right has to be earned every single minute of your life. That means getting the best education as possible, so you can think critically and express yourself clearly. Get a good job, and support yourself.

PAYING FORWARD BLESSINGS

You see a young woman walking minding her own business. You run after her. You approach her. You get her defense down. After you get her defense down you go and get what you want and leave her with 3 or 5 kids and you go to the next young woman. You do the same thing. You keep going, breaking them down. You are breaking a whole village down. What king of legacy is this? What kind of legacy do you want to leave behind?

Nowadays in South Sudan it is hard for a female to get a job, if you don't know anyone that works in the government. Otherwise you must let your body be available to those who will hire you so you can get a job and that is sexual abuse. I want human rights recognized in South Sudan. I want those young fourteen year old girls to be heard. I want them to feel safe at home. It is awful when the fourteen year old girls go to sleep at night afraid. I want them to go to sleep without dreaming about a man breaking through their window in the night to get them pregnant.

In Africa today the young girls are suffering from harassment and non-freedom. A 14 year-old girl marrying a 60 year old man because that man said so. This needs to stop right here, right now. This is the time for us to change. It is time to tell your brothers, sisters, daughters, and sons to go in the right direction. It is time for us to start moving in the right direction. Leave this world with a positive attitude in peace. Those young girls deserve a better life. They need a better future. You might see a fourteen year old girl wearing a ring on the wrong finger cause she did not even have anyone teaching her what the right finger for the ring was.

You get what you want ... and leave her. Then you go to the next girl and use her as well. You keep going through your life breaking down a thousand girls. Breaking the world down like that, what kind of a legacy will you leave?

I am asking all those men to consider what they are doing to the future. I am asking them to change this future. Maybe I can only get one man to pay more respect to those girls, but one man is a start. Just because all your buddies are behaving badly I am pleading with you to be different. If just one man shows women more respect in South Sudan then it is a start. Make sure the legacy you leave behind is one that you can be proud of.

You ask, "Why should I do this?" My answer is to ask God what He wants you to do. God is a God of love. What do you think He would want you to do? Do not believe what others say. Be strong. Do a good deed. Do not ask for reward. If you do many good deeds you will have a positive influence and someone will *pay it forward.*

Never hurt others. Play smart, don't play rough. If you don't play smart, your tongue could slowly kill yourself and others. Your tongue can damage your life. Just because other men say to do this does not mean it is good. Use your own mind and heart to decide what is good. Sometimes you have to be careful making decisions using other's ideas, because some ideas are good and some are bad. Your fingers are not the same as ideas, so be careful what your fingers do. Remember we are all human beings. Many people have trouble because sometimes you don't recognize these things.

People who take advantage of others and hurt people need to think about their own lives. You can't go back in time and undo that time when someone hurt you or your loved one, but you can stop yourself from hurting someone else. People who are hurt try to hurt others so that everyone feels the same. That has to stop.

If you keep trying to hurt people who hurt you, you won't have time to love people who love you. Living in fear is not going to do you any good. Just let it go and leave it alone because this moment is for you. Being confident and positive can help you in life. You are not alone. You have Heavenly Father listening to you all the time.

The worst thing that can happen to a good person is they die. Once that happens they can't be hurt again. I would rather stand before God and say I died trying to do well than confessing I hurt others deliberately. So I hope and pray at least one man in South Sudan will try to do good instead of hurting the lives of those young girls.

Nobody knows what will happen tomorrow nor will anyone know the destination of anyone's life. Even if people criticize you for doing good, maybe their criticism doesn't matter because life is temporary. After all, sometimes you have to be better than others.

It is so sad when some people don't get what they want and then they blame it on others and God. If God created you as a healthy person with everything needed, meaning two hands, two legs, two eyes, and everything else, then it's up to you to make something of your life. Stop blaming your own problems on others because the whole world is going wrong. You don't need to be perfect but you do need to be more confident because confidence is the key of everything in the human life.

Confidence makes you take the next step forward when you can't see where you are going. Confidence is what drives you to reach success and not give up.

You use bad manners in your everyday life and when others are using those same bad manners you get offended because you are not confident in your own behavior. How long are you going to hold on to some little offense or be mad about it? That's the history of humanity and you can't get rid of it. It's just like a permanent tattoo. In order for you to get rid of permanent tattoo you have to cover it up. So in order for us to do better as a people, you certainly don't need to fall back in time because of history. You can't be happy with saying instead, "Yes, life has got me down a few times. And it's done it again." You have to move forward with your life.

Everything happens for a reason. You laugh today you cry tomorrow. Then you remember the person that you treated badly. That's why you need to be careful of how you treat other people. Don't look down on people. No one knows the destination of life. The only one who has control of your life plan is God. You don't get what you want all the time. You don't know why, other than it's your plan of life.

Life can be tough sometimes and that's why it is important to have both parents in a child's life so you can plan life together. Do your best by providing everything a child should have from their parents and leave the rest to God.

ACHIEVING SUCCESS

Success is a mindset you don't need to clear with anybody. It is all yours. You can start the process of changing today. All you need to do is change your mindset.

Everyone has the gift necessary to become a success. This gift is powered by your natural ability and skills. Your gift will make room for you wherever you want to place yourself. Pursue your dream.

Sometimes people try to do something they are not suited to do. People see someone with a big car or a fancy house and they want that for themselves. Trying to be someone else is not following your gift. Don't go against your gift.

I wanted something straight up here. I had a lot of people saying: "Be Your Own Boss -- don't work for somebody -- don't be an employee." They want everyone to be the boss! But it's impossible not to have employees in this Earth. Because whatever you have, if you own the hospital, you will still need a housekeeper to keep the floor clean; someone who can do the laundry; someone who can make food for a patient. You will need employees otherwise you would never run a business. Without employees it's impossible. It is like somebody saying, "I can stand on the air without touching the floor." That's why it's important before you speak to think first.

How do you achieve success?

Preparation + Opportunity + Hard Work + God = Success

If you want success, you can't leave out one part. Especially, don't forget hard work.

Learn how to be honest with yourself. Little things lead you to big things. You get started with a red light so obey the law. Being impatient and running the light is not being wise. Obey God. Because you are brand new when you are put together, your body will function right. The way God made you. When you wait for the green light you can go home safe, but when you cheat you think, "it's a red light and nobody's watching, so why don't I just go?" But just because you don't see a car coming, you never know when a car will come. It is especially dangerous because the other cars, they've got the right-of-way, they will be coming fast, you can get killed. So if you cheated and did not obey the law, you weren't being honest with yourself.

EXERCISES

1. Where were you when you were eighteen years old?

2. Were you prepared to support yourself when you were eighteen? Were you prepared to support a family? Write here what advice you would give a teenager.

AYAK'S WISDOM

1. I can't get a job because I do not have a good education.

   I didn't have a good education. I was born during the civil war of 1984 in South Sudan. My father was taken away from me and my mother took me and my four siblings to North Sudan. She started working as a mid-wife, and cleaning houses. She couldn't afford to put us in school so that's why I didn't have enough education. So I want to leave this message to the next generation that education is the key to success but even if you do not have a good education do not give up.

2. How do I get an education? I am on my own and I am an adult.

   Talk to people at the nearest school and they will help you get an advisor. In the United States your advisor will usually be able to help get you enrolled in school at no cost to you. They will also give you advice on how to support yourself while you are in school. If you are willing to work hard and not give up, you will succeed. I am not saying it will be easy. Success requires hard work.

3. Should I make goals? How do you do that?

   Set your goals when you wake up in the morning. Focus on your soul. No one is in charge on your own happiness, or your life, except you.

4. What kind of goals should I set?

   Never be afraid to try something new because life gets in the way all the time. Keep going. Invest in yourself and believe in yourself. Sometimes you don't see results right away. Keep going until you see the results. Results will not come if you quit. Keep learning until you get to the next level. It takes courage, tears, and pain to reach the sky. No matter how much it hurts.

   Remember everyone has different talents. Not everyone can do everything well.

10

REMEMBERING WE ARE GOD'S CHILDREN

"Your heavenly father and his beloved son love you perfectly. They would not require you to experience a moment more of difficulty than is absolutely needed for your personal benefit or for that of those you love."

— Richard G. Scott

FORGIVING

Forgive people for what they have done wrong to you so you can be free because if you don't forgive them you will be living the same darkness as them. Sometimes when you step on someone's feet they can't move and you can't either. Now you're both stuck. But as soon as you move your feet you are both free to go. So forgiveness is not just for the person, it's for you as well.

- Always keep your mouth in order so you don't open the door for your enemies.
- Recognize the interaction between spiritual law and natural law.
- I'm glad Jesus never says "This is the last time I will forgive you."

- To gain Jesus' forgiveness, you must start with a clean heart.
- You must repent of the things you know are wrong.
- Then begin by forgiving yourself.

EVERYTHING THAT GOD MADE

Everything that God made has value. He made everything of value hard to get. If you want oil you have to drill into the ground sometimes miles to extract the most precious drops of oil. If you want diamonds you have to dig deep into the side of a mountain with hopes to uncover one.

The most precious gifts that God has given us are his children. You have to treat them with love and understanding. Talk to your children. Don't just order them around. If you order them around they will disobey you every chance they get. If you love them and show them that you love them and take good care of them and set good examples for them, they will try the best they can to make you proud of them. Do not belittle them or blame them if they have difficulties. Love them and help them understand that even when they try their best things do not always go perfectly. Let them know that you love them for their own special qualities. Not all children are the same but all children deserve the same love and gentle understanding.

EVERYBODY'S LIFE MATTERS

Everybody's lives matter. I don't want the future generation to go through what I went through. Not again. We have to remember this when we provide aid. No child deserves more help than another. We cannot forget a child because we do not know how to help that child. Sometimes we have to take that extra step to help someone. Everybody's lives matter. Now I talk about helping children, because that is the future. That does not mean we should ignore the adults. Everybody's lives matter. But it is the adults who we have to take under our wing and teach them how to treat our children and each other. It is the adults who are hard to teach. If we can get the adults to stop killing each other we will have done a remarkable thing.

LOOKING AT THE WORLD

The world is catching on fire sooner than I thought. So many nations are being plagued by war, disaster and disease that there is much work to be done. Some people say, "We can't save everyone." I think we can. We just have to do it right. We have to bring up new leaders to increase our effort. Our children will be the leaders of our future. We have to help as many as we can so that our love will spread over the entire world.

LOOKING AT THE FUTURE

I see the light in the future generation -- I see the changing. And I say let the new generation take over because, with them, you can fix it. Any more you mess with the world trying to fix it, the more you mess the world up. Instead of messing with it, help the children change. When the glass is broke it is hard to put it back, but it'll be easy to buy a new glass. So let's have the new generation design a new glass.

So this is the way I see the world and to do my best to try to help I created Ayak's Helping Hands. This is how I do my best. Each child I can help is one more positive influence in the world who can help other children when they grow up. Every child that grows up loved is one less problem in this troubled world.

EXERCISES

1. What are your goals to improve your life?

____

____

____

____

____

____

2. How have you prepared yourself to accomplish these goals? List a couple of things you have already done to accomplish these goals?

____

____

____

____

____

____

____

AYAK'S WISDOM

1. What can you do when the forces against peace and love are overwhelming?

   You can't stand against it but you can walk beside it. In other words, don't give up. Walk forward. Never retreat. Always keep good goals in your heart and never betray those good goals.

2. How do you know your goals are good?

   You can only know this in your heart. Never try to fulfill a goal be doing something unloving. All your actions must be loving. Keep all your goals loving. Never say a bad action was done for love or by love. There is no love in any bad action. I pray about every decision and listen for God's approval through the testimony of the Holy Ghost. I learned to do this in my church. It works.

3. What can you do when events are overwhelming?

   The society you live in today is confusing -- even the weather is confusing. In the morning you wait for the Sun. If you're not being yourself, you will be confused. You won't even know day and night; because you won't know where you are. You need to believe in God first. You need to believe that God has a plan and that His plan is the best plan possible. There are reasons why bad things happen. Don't get caught up in the bad things. Just be stubborn in the good things. Do not let go of what is right and know in your heart that things will get better. One day you will wake up and see the sun and know that it is a good day.

11

CREATING AYAK'S HOPE

"My beloved brothers and sisters, fear not. Be of good cheer. The future is as bright as your faith."

— Thomas S. Monson

CREATING AYAK'S HOPE

Being a leader of my tribe gives me many responsibilities. It is my duty to try to help my people. The people of my birth nation call me "Mother of South Sudan." They rely on me to help them. I created my website, "Ayak's Hope" as the main site to distribute information on what I am doing to help my people. My organization is called "Ayak's Helping Hands."

I see people in trouble all around the world so I do not think it is enough to just help the Dinka people. I want to help all people around the world. I go to South Sudan to defend my people every year that I can. On those years when I cannot go myself my team provides our help.

So now if a woman or girl has a job in South Sudan, to get that job now, you must sleep with the person who hires you. It is that hard for a woman to get a job in South Sudan. In order for a female to get a job you had to do that. That's how bad it was and that's how bad it is now in 2021.

My mission is to help people around the world, though mostly in South Sudan. That's why I created Ayaks Helping Hands. The goal is to build schools and healthcare centers throughout South Sudan. We want at-risk people from South Sudan to have an opportunity to attend schools and to have access to basic medical care.

Ayaks Helping Hands is led by myself and two other people who lived in South Sudan and are acutely aware of the needs of people there. With the dedication of these two individuals our work has begun. Imagine how contributions from people around the world will enable South Sudan to become a safer and better place for the people. I am the "Founder and Activist" and supporting me is Akuch Madut as Vice President and Jok Biong Kuol as Director of Education.

Each year I gather together the donations made to my organization and buy supplies which I take to my people. The supplies I take to the Abyei Area are almost entirely medical supplies and school supplies because these provide the most effective aid to the children.

The future of the Dinka people is in the children. The more educated, the more protected, the healthier they are, the more hope there is for the future. To accomplish this we have two main teams: *Life Saving Task Force* and *Tomorrow's Hope Scholarship*.

LIFE SAVING TASKFORCE

To carry out the medical aid goals we support a **Life Saving Task Force** to treat people who are suffering with typhoid and malaria in South Sudan. It provides basic health care to take blood tests and to test for malaria, and typhoid.

Our goal is to save lives and inspire health in our communities by connecting people to a healthier environment. Our purpose is to build a better future with our values, which are hope, empowerment, and fairness. Life Saving is funded by contributions to support our important work. We advocate, we listen, and we lead. Since 2018 LSTF has been a beacon of help to all people affected by malaria and typhoid.

We are providing medical personnel and medical supplies for treating people. We are securing partnerships and grants from medical companies to donate supplies and equipment. Our medical team has treated 3000 people so far.

PROVIDING EDUCATION

Our second team provides **Tomorrow's Hope Scholarship**. We provide a scholarship for those who are not able to pay for their education. Our scholarship covers the areas of South Sudan, and Cairo, Egypt. Our scholarship covers a full education from elementary school to college and university studies.

The application process begins with an essay with additional documents to support the application as they become available. The essay is to help us get to know the applicant. What personal qualities make the student a good candidate for a Tomorrow's Hope Scholarship? We especially want to know of any experience these new students have volunteering or serving others in their community. Our Director of Educational Services is Jok Biong. To make this a reality we are building schools.

We already have one school completed and the second school in progress. School supplies have been donated and are ready to ship. We plan to hire additional teachers and obtain additional much-needed school supplies as we are able.

GROWING FOOD FOR THE FUTURE

Ayaks Helping Hands sponsors **AHH Hope Gardens** to help feed the people of South Sudan. We aspire to turn compassion into action so that all people affected by disaster in South Sudan receive harvest crops. Around May every year we are going to plant wheat, corn, okra, pepper and more. As seen in the accompanying photos the first year was very successful.

PROVIDING ADDITIONAL SERVICES

We also provide these additional Services: Foster Care, Child Care Services, Domestic Violence Shelters, Men Shelters, Youth Programs for Ages 10 to 18, Back-to-school Preparation, and Preschooling.

We have conducted Back to School Night each year to provide needed school supplies in Sudan and Mexico.

In 2011 we built our first school. Shown above is our bus loaded with $30,000 worth of school supplies in 2017. This was repeated in 2018. In 2018 we worked with governor Qwan and his minister to expand services.

EXERCISES

1. What have you done to help your own children to grow up as responsible loving adults?

____

____

____

____

____

2. Consider your own life, what have you done to help the children of the world?

____

____

____

____

____

3. Now that you have finished my book, how do you want to love and serve the world? Compare your answer here to your answer at the end of Chapter One. How have you changed?

____

____

____

____

____

AYAK'S WISDOM

1. How can I help?

   With your help, we can make a difference in the world.

   We look forward to sharing news and stories about Ayaks Helping Hands and the work we do to help around the world.

   Look at our website and leave a donation or call us for further information.

A Final Note

Now What? Now that you have read and finished my book, what actions are you going to take? What goals are you going to set? Now that you have read my book you know that positive thoughts yield positive attitudes. A happy approach to life yields happiness even when things are bad. A loving approach to life fills your heart with love so that you can share that love with children in need. Healing the world is accomplished one child at a time. If you provide service or funds to Ayak's Helping Hands you will be helping not only the children in Ayak's schools and hospitals, but you will be helping those children to grow up to provide further help to thousands of future children. I challenge you to take action! Knowledge is not power, "applied" knowledge is power. You can read all the books in this world about positive thinking but if you don't apply the wisdom in this book you will not be bringing hope to these children.

In the ten exercise lines below list your ten actions that you commit to taking within the next year as a result of reading this book.

1. ______________________________

2. ______________________________

3. ______________________________

4. ______________________________

5. ______________________________

6. ______________________________

7. ______________________________

8. ______________________________

9. ______________________________

10. ______________________________

In this book you learned that survival does not come easily. It requires work, hard work. It also requires a positive attitude and faith in God. You cannot give up. Survival is a daily struggle. You may say, "It is not worth it" but giving up will not solve anything. Saying, "I am not strong enough" will not get the job done. If you focus your energy you will survive. No matter how bleak life looks as your world falls apart around you and everything you worked for in your life falls away into nothing, there is always hope. Never lose your hope. Cling to hope and take one step at a time. Ask God to help but do not be surprised you do not hear an answer or bad things continue to happen in your life. Always remember yours is not the only life in this world that is out of control. God will help you if you are faithful to Him, but His help may come in unexpected ways and at unexpected times. Sometimes the thing you need the most is not what you want. Do not lose faith and hope when God directs you along a thorny path. You may not find an escape route to North Sudan, Egypt, and then to the United States where you find the loving support you had prayed for. Instead your path to safety may be totally unexpected.

Now that you have read my book, I encourage you to contact me and tell me what you liked about my book and what you disliked so I can improve it for the next printing.

More importantly tell me about you, your challenges, your obstacles and adversities, so I can help you. In fact, I would like to offer you a complimentary, no obligation 30-60 minute consultation by phone, text, or in person (if geography allows) to see how I can help and assist you. So please email me, or better yet text me with your name, your time zone and we will schedule your complimentary consultation.

Websites

ayakshope.org

facebook.com/groups/274506573243916l/?ref=share

Email

letusknow@ayakshope.org

Ayaks Helpings Hands is a 501 (c) (3) organization with EIN#82-2127624. Your generous tax-deductible contribution is very much needed to complete our mission. Ayaks Helping Hands was organized to support other 501 (c) (3) organizations including, but not limited to, educational organizations, religious organizations, and environmental preservation organizations as determined by the board of directors.

PS…I wish you good luck! I wish you success and prosperity! I wish you all the success in the world.

Your friend Ayak Mithyang

ABOUT THE AUTHOR

AYAK MITHYANG is an international philanthropist and professional care-giver, providing teachers doctors and supplies to the children of the war torn countries in the world. She grew up as a native African in South Sudan. She lost her parents and fled South Sudan as a refugee. She has formed her organization, Ayak's Helping Hands, to prevent the cycle of abuse from dragging new generations of children into civil and tribal wars. As director of her charitable organization she has provided education and health care for thousands of children, primarily in South Sudan and Mexico. Her organization has three divisions: the Life Saving Task Force provides hospitals, doctors and medical aid; Tomorrow's Hope Scholarship provides scholarships for students who need support; and Ayaks Helping Hands Hope Gardens in South Sudan provides farm plots and supplies for growing food on farms. In addition her organization provides supplies to the schools and libraries where she is able. A typical supply run delivers $10,000 worth of school supplies. She is currently soliciting further donations to expand her efforts. A Dinka speaker, she went to school in Sudan and learned Arabic. She immigrated to the United States from Egypt and has been living in California and Washington for seventeen years.

Made in the USA
Columbia, SC
02 December 2021

50259185R00071